RIVER
ADVENTURES

MISSISSIPPI

W
FRANKLIN WATTS
LONDON • SYDNEY

First published 2012 by Franklin Watts
Hachette Children's Books
338 Euston Road
London NW1 3BH

Franklin Watts Australia
Level 17/207 Kent Street
Sydney, NSW 2000

© Franklin Watts 2012

Design, editing, picture research by Paul Manning
Proofreading by Alice Harman

Produced for Franklin Watts by
White-Thomson Publishing Ltd

www.wtpub.co.uk
+44 (0) 845 362 8240

A CIP catalogue record for this book is available
from the British Library.

ISBN 978 1 4451 1040 0

Dewey classification: 917.6'2

Key to images

Top cover image: The skyline of Minneapolis
Main cover image: Cargo ships on the Mississippi
Previous page: A North American bald eagle
This page: Panorama of St Anthony Falls, Minneapolis

Note to Teachers and Parents
Every effort has been made to ensure that the websites
listed on page 32 are suitable for children, that they are of
the highest educational value, and that they contain no
inappropriate or offensive material. However, because of the
nature of the internet, it is impossible to guarantee that
the content of these sites will not be altered. We strongly
recommend that internet access is supervised by
a responsible adult.

Printed in China

Franklin Watts is a division of Hachette
Children's Books, an Hachette UK company
www.hachette.co.uk

Picture Credits
t = top, b = bottom, l = left, r = right

Front cover, Shutterstock/Ed Metz; title page, Shutterstock/Lori Skelton;
2-3, Wikimedia/Bobak Ha'Eri; 4, Dreamstime/David Mcshane; 5t (map),
Paul Manning; 5b, Dreamstime/John James Henderson; 6, Dreamstime/
Ben Zastovnik; 7b, Shutterstock/Deborah McCague; 7t, Peter Frischmuth/
argus/Still Pictures; 8, Shutterstock/Iofoto; 9t, Shutterstock/Tyler Olson;
9b, Dreamstime/Eldancer1; 10, Wikimedia/Ronfar623; 11t, Shutterstock/
Scott Milless; 11b, Wikimedia/Howard Morland; 12, Wikimedia/Pyrokat;
13t, Wikimedia/John Polo; 13b, Courtesy Mill City Museum, Minneapolis;
14, Shutterstock/Ed Metz; 15t, Dreamstime/Czuber; 15b, Shutterstock/
Karla Caspari; 16, Wikimedia/Daniel Ramirez; 17l, US Army Corps of
Engineers Digital Visual Library; 17r, Wikimedia/Robert Lawton; 18,
Shutterstock/Kavram; 19t, Shutterstock/Patrick Poendl; 19b, Agricultural
Research Service/US Dept of Agriculture; 20, Getty/Scott Olson; 21t,
US Army Corps of Engineers; 21b, Dreamstime/Anne Power; 22, David
Nance/Agricultural Research Service/US Dept of Agriculture; 22 inset,
Shutterstock/Laurin Rinder; 23t, Shutterstock/Henryk Sadura; 23b,
Bettmann/Corbis; 24-5, Shutterstock/Henryk Sadura; 25t, Shutterstock/
Ed Metz; 26, Dreamstime/Paula Stephens; 27t, NPL/Gerrit Vyn; 27b,
Dreamstime/Asterixvs; 28, Corbis/Danny Lehman; 29t, Getty/Mario
Tama; 29b, Dreamstime/Steve Allen; 31a, Shutterstock/Scott Prokop; 31b,
Shutterstock/REDAV; 31c, Shutterstock/Al Mueller; 31d, Shutterstock/
ckchiu; 31e, Shutterstock/Richard Goldberg; 31f, Shutterstock/LacoKozyna;
31g, Shutterstock/Brian Lasenby.

CONTENTS

A Mississippi Journey

The Mississippi River flows for 4,104 km (2,550 miles) from Minnesota in the northern USA to the Gulf of Mexico. Although it is not the longest US river (the Missouri is longer), it is the most important route for ships and transport. You will follow the river from its source to the sea.

A mighty river

▼ The Mississippi floodplain contains the richest farmland in the United States.

The Mississippi is like the United States itself: vast, powerful and always changing. The river has played a vital part in the country's history. People have used it for transport, farming and industry since ancient times. It is one of the busiest working rivers in the world, carrying boats loaded with goods and raw materials from all over the American continent.

Map labels:

SASKATCHEWAN
CANADA
MONTANA
NORTH DAKOTA
MISSOURI RIVER
Lake Itasca
MINNESOTA
Coon Rapids
WYOMING
Minneapolis • St Paul
MISSISSIPPI RIVER
WISCONSIN
SOUTH DAKOTA
MISSOURI RIVER
ROCKY MOUNTAINS
NEBRASKA
Des Moines
Omaha
Chicago
IOWA
GREAT PLAINS
ILLINOIS
COLORADO
Kansas City
Springfield
INDIANA
KANSAS
St Louis
UNITED STATES
MISSOURI
KENTUCKY
OKLAHOMA
Oklahoma City
ARKANSAS
MISSISSIPPI RIVER
Memphis
TENNESSEE
TEXAS
ALABAMA
GEORGIA
MISSISSIPPI
Baton Rouge
LOUISIANA
New Orleans
MEXICO
Gulf of Mexico

N W E S

Birth of a river

The Mississippi River was formed during the last Ice Age, 10–12,000 years ago. At that time, most of the Earth was covered with glaciers. When the ice melted, water flowed across the land, forming the Mississippi channel. The name 'Mississippi' comes from Native American words meaning 'Big River'.

▼ This bald eagle lives by catching fish in the Mississippi. It uses its powerful talons to snatch fish from the river.

Mississippi wildlife

The Mississippi is home to about 240 species of fish and 50 different mammals. Moose and eagles live along the upper reaches of the river. The bald eagle is the national symbol of the United States, and is a protected species. Alligators and muskrats make their homes in the lower Mississippi.

The River Source

The place where a river begins is called its source. The source of the Mississippi is Lake Itasca in northern Minnesota. Here, the river starts life as a small, clear stream flowing out of the lake.

▼ At Lake Itasca in Minnesota, a wooden post and a line of stepping stones mark the spot where the Mississippi begins.

Lake Itasca is shallow and surrounded by pine forests. Many tourists come here to see where the Mississippi begins.

As the stream heads south, it twists and turns through lakes and marshes and over waterfalls. There are few towns or cities here, but the area is popular with tourists for walking, camping and fishing. There are also special lands, called reserves, for Native American groups such as the Ojibwe, who live close to the river's source.

▶ Minnesota has nearly 12,000 lakes. They are popular for canoeing and fishing.

Hunter-gatherers

Roughly 7–8,000 years ago, tribes such as the Ojibwe hunted wild animals for food by the river. These early people lay in wait for bison, deer and moose at the water's edge, and killed them with stone-tipped spears.

Later, other Native American groups arrived in the region. They built larger, more permanent settlements, and made a variety of stone, wood and bone tools. The ancient burial mounds they left behind can still be seen at Lake Itasca's Indian Cemetery.

The mound builders

Long ago, America's first farming peoples lived alongside the Mississippi. Because of the earthen mounds they left behind, they are sometimes known as the 'mound builders'. Some mounds supported temples. Others were used as burial sites. They continued to be built until as late as the 16th century.

▶ Burial mounds dating back to prehistoric times can be found throughout the Mississippi valley.

The Upper River

YOU ARE HERE

You are now travelling the Upper Mississippi. This reaches from the source at Lake Itasca to where the Mississippi meets the Missouri north of St Louis.

▼ The Mississippi is a vital transport route for industry. Fleets of flat-bottomed boats called barges carry all kinds of goods, from flour and corn to coal, iron, steel and timber.

The river highway

On the Mississippi, the channel used by boats is at least 2.7 m (9 ft) deep throughout its length. To keep it open, sediment has to be cleared from the river bed by special boats called dredgers. Between Lake Itasca and St Louis, a system of dams is also used to make sure that there is always enough water in the channel for boats (*see pages 10–11*).

◀ The huge prairie that stretches across the Upper Mississippi is known as America's 'corn belt'. As well as corn, soya is an important crop here.

Clear water

The upper river is mostly clear of silt. Its colour does not change until it meets the muddy-red waters of the Missouri further south. It flows through rolling hills, marshland and flat grassland called prairie. The soils are fertile, and farmers grow corn and wheat beside the river. Forests of pine, maple, oak and hickory also grow here.

River wildlife

The Upper Mississippi is home to many wild animals. Black bears wait on the banks to catch fish in the river, while deer, moose and beavers hunt for food in the forest. Millions of migrating birds also use the river on their journeys between Canada and the United States. Their migration route is called the Mississippi flyway.

▶ Black bears are the commonest type in North America. They grow to about 1.5 to 1.8 m (5 or 6 ft) tall and weigh 90–270 kg (200–600 lb).

Dams and Locks

YOU ARE HERE

At Coon Rapids, named for the raccoons once found there, you stop to explore one of the many dams on the Upper Mississippi.

Controlling the river

Dams hold back the water and form a deeper channel so that boats can travel up and down the river. They also allow water to be stored in reservoirs. This water can then be used for irrigating fields or be released back into the river if the water level is low. The first dams were built on the Upper Mississippi in the 1880s. Later, more dams were built between Minneapolis and St Louis.

▼ Coon Rapids Dam was originally built to provide hydroelectric power for homes and factories. Today, the dam reservoir is mainly used for recreation.

◀ A barge enters a lock chamber on the Mississippi. When the lock gates are shut, the water level inside the chamber can be raised or lowered.

Locks

South of Minneapolis, locks were built to allow barges to bypass the dams and travel all the way up and down the river. The locks work like lifts, raising or lowering the water level, so that boats can transfer safely to the next stretch of river.

Beside the locks, there are also pools and reservoirs. These are widely used for recreation. Each year, millions of people visit the pools to camp, picnic, go boating or watch wildlife.

What is a wing dam?

A wing dam is a barrier that only extends partway into a river. Its job is to force water into a fast-moving centre channel and to stop sediment building up on the river bed. The Mississippi has thousands of wing dams. Many are below the surface of the water, and can sometimes be a hazard for boats.

▶ Canoeists avoid a wing dam on a man-made section of the river bed.

YOU ARE HERE

The Twin Cities

At Minneapolis, you reach the first city on your journey. Together with its twin city, St Paul, Minneapolis is home to 3.6 million people. The two cities directly border each other. Their central or 'downtown' districts are about 14 km (9 miles) apart.

A mill town

The city of Minneapolis grew up where the Mississippi is joined by the Minnesota River. In the early days, water from the St Anthony Falls *(below)* provided energy for local industries. The river also provided the transport route for bringing raw materials into the city, and taking finished goods out.

▼ *The St Anthony Falls at Minneapolis are the only natural waterfalls on the river.*

◀ This photo of St Paul, Minnesota, was taken in winter. At this time of year, parts of the river sometimes freeze over completely.

Thanks to the river and the railways, Minneapolis quickly grew into a thriving mill town. Huge farms in the north-west grew wheat. Their harvests were transported into the city on hundreds of rail wagons.

A financial centre

Today, most of the city's wealth comes from financial services. However, in the Mill City Museum and the restored waterfront area, you can still see reminders of the days when Minneapolis was a busy industrial centre.

Water power

Above St Anthony Falls, water was diverted from the Mississippi into a system of canals, and used to turn wooden waterwheels. These provided the energy for saw mills, flour mills and paper mills. Sometimes, so much water was diverted from the river that the St Anthony Falls ran dry!

▶ The stern wheel of a Mississippi steamboat stands outside the Mill City Museum in Minneapolis.

The Working River

Beyond Minneapolis, the Mississippi widens. Between here and St Louis, it is joined by the Minnesota, Wisconsin, Illinois and Missouri rivers. Together, they form one of the world's great transport networks.

YOU ARE HERE

▼ A single towboat (right of picture) steers a fleet of more than 50 barges on the river north of St Louis.

A cargo route

The Mississippi has been a cargo route for more than 200 years. Large boats began carrying lumber, cotton and other goods up and down the river in the 1800s. Today, about 159 million tonnes of cargo are carried by Mississippi barges each year.

◀ Mississippi steamboats were once a common sight on the river. Today, replica boats like this are used for tourist cruises.

The steamboat era

In 1811, the first Mississippi steamboat, the New Orleans. *travelled from Pittsburgh to New Orleans to test the waters for navigation. By 1860, there were more than 1,000 steamboats on the river. The steamboat boom brought prosperity to many cities, but within a few years the arrival of the railways brought the steamboat age to an end.*

Steamboats and barges

In early times, Native American trappers used canoes to carry furs to trading posts along the river. Later, steamboats were used on the river. With their powerful engines, steamboats could travel against the current. This meant that they could carry goods and passengers the length of the river.

Nowadays, fleets of barges travel the Mississippi. Carrying goods by barge is environmentally-friendly and cost-effective. A single barge can carry 1,500 tonnes of cargo. It would take 15 railway wagons or 58 trucks to transport the same load.

▼ Tough diesel-engined towboats have taken the place of steamboats on the river.

15

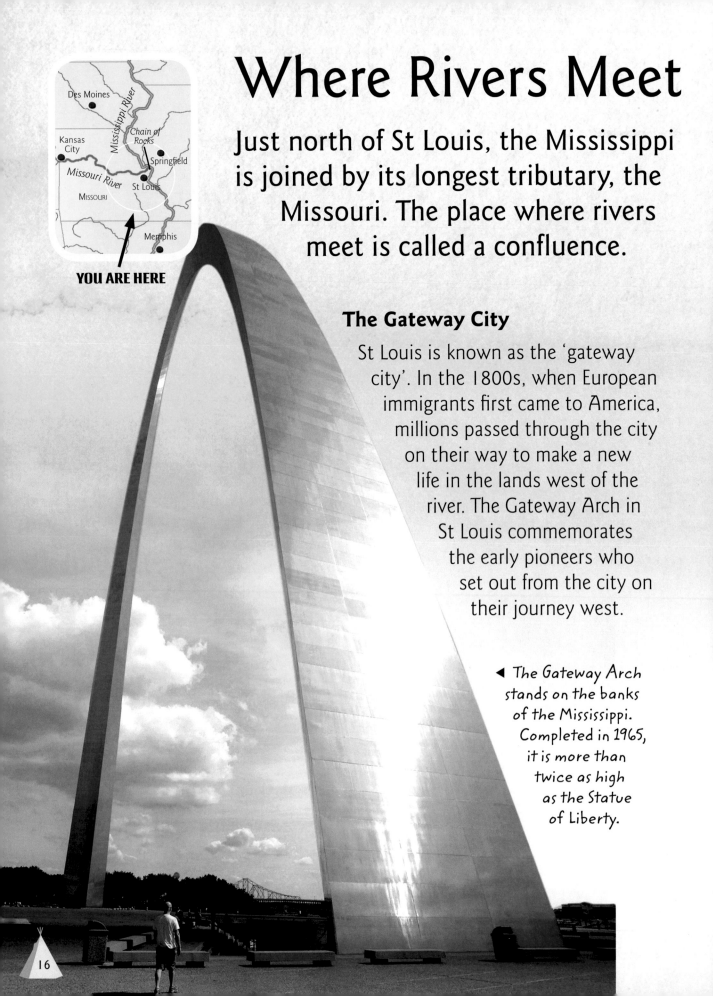

Where Rivers Meet

Just north of St Louis, the Mississippi is joined by its longest tributary, the Missouri. The place where rivers meet is called a confluence.

YOU ARE HERE

The Gateway City

St Louis is known as the 'gateway city'. In the 1800s, when European immigrants first came to America, millions passed through the city on their way to make a new life in the lands west of the river. The Gateway Arch in St Louis commemorates the early pioneers who set out from the city on their journey west.

◀ The Gateway Arch stands on the banks of the Mississippi. Completed in 1965, it is more than twice as high as the Statue of Liberty.

◄ South of the Mississippi–Missouri confluence, this canal was built to allow river traffic to bypass the rapids known as the 'Chain of Rocks' (below).

A trading hub

Because it lies close to the meeting point of two rivers, St Louis has always been an important transport and trading point. In the early days, pioneers stopped here to buy equipment and supplies before making the long trek west. Later, steamboats boosted trade on the river, and the city grew into a major port.

St Louis today

Today, the St Louis area is home to more than 2.8 million people. The port is still one of its busiest areas, stretching for 115 km (70 miles) on either side of the river. The port contains 134 piers, wharves and docks, as well as 55 'fleeting areas' where barges wait for towboats to take them downriver.

The 'Chain of Rocks'

After meeting the Missouri, the Mississippi sweeps round in a 15-km (9.3-mile) curve known as the 'Chain of Rocks'. The rapids here were so dangerous for boats that in 1940 a canal was built to bypass them. The canal stretches 12.8 km (8 miles), rejoining the Mississippi just north of downtown St Louis.

YOU ARE HERE

The Missouri

At St Louis, you make a detour to explore the Missouri River. Although the Missouri is a tributary of the Mississippi, it is the longest river in North America.

The Rocky Mountains

The Missouri starts its journey in the Rocky Mountains of Montana. Here it tumbles over rapids and waterfalls, cutting deep gorges through the rock. Later, it reaches the flatter lands of the Great Plains and widens out into a series of lakes. This is the corn and cattle country of America's Mid-West.

▼ The Missouri River flows through the Rocky Mountains of northern Montana.

▶ The Missouri is sometimes known as the 'Big Muddy' because of the rich brown sediment that colours its waters.

The Great Plains

Before the arrival of European settlers, the Great Plains were home to more than a million Native Americans. Tribes such as the Blackfoot, Comanche and Cheyenne lived here in tents called tepees. They moved from place to place, following the huge herds of deer and bison that roamed the prairie.

From the 1700s onwards, the Plains tribes were steadily hunted down and driven off their lands by white settlers.

Wheat country

For a century or more, the Great Plains were intensively farmed. Nowadays, the region is still the main source of wheat for the USA, but many farmers are leaving it. As people drift away to the towns, the prairies are once again being turned over to buffalo herds.

Missouri mud

As the Missouri flows south, it brings with it sediment, made up of mud and stones carried down from the mountains. When the river floods, the sediment, or silt, is left behind on the floodplain. In the past, the silt created rich farmland. Nowadays, much of it ends up trapped behind giant dams further upstream.

▶ Bison gave Native Americans meat, skins for clothing and shelter, and bones to make tools.

Flood Alert!

Back on the Mississippi, you reach the lower river. Here, heavy spring rains and quickly melting snow can cause devastating floods.

The map shows:
Missouri River, Illinois, Springfield, St Louis, Ohio River, Missouri, Tennessee, Memphis, Mississippi River

YOU ARE HERE

▼ Tennessee residents paddle a boat through a flooded neighbourhood in May 2011.

The floodwaters are often brought to the river by its tributaries, the Ohio and Missouri rivers. The river basin soaks up some of the water. But if the soil becomes saturated, the water rushes down the tributaries to the main stream, which bursts its banks and floods the land.

◄ This barrier, known as the Morganza Spillway, can be opened to divert water from the Mississippi when the river is in flood. The spillway allows the floodwater to flow safely out into the Gulf of Mexico.

A great flood

Between April and May 2011, huge storms dumped record rainfall on the Mississippi Basin, causing some of the biggest floods for nearly a hundred years. Crops and livestock were destroyed. Many people had to leave their homes when floodwaters were diverted to protect the cities of New Orleans and Baton Rouge.

Levées

Along the banks of the Mississippi, sloping walls called levées *(right)* have been built to keep the river from overflowing. Altogether, the levées on the Mississippi stretch for more than 5,600 km (3,500 miles). The levées reduce the impact of floods, but do not remove the danger completely.

Levées

Levées help to prevent flooding by containing the flow of a river within low mounds or embankments. Because they tend to make a river flow faster, levées can make flooding more likely at other points of the river. For this reason, once one levée is built, others have to be built at all low points of the river system.

Cotton Country

YOU ARE HERE

After meeting the Ohio River, the Mississippi slows and widens. The rich soils and warm, wet climate make this area ideal for growing cotton.

Memphis

In the 19th century, the city of Memphis was a centre of the cotton trade. Its great advantage was its location on the Mississippi River. This made it easy to transport cotton to Europe, and to the northern and eastern USA. The city became so famous as a cotton town that it was known as 'King Cotton'.

▼ Harvesting cotton with a combine harvester. The seed heads that contain the cotton (inset) are stripped from the stems, which are thrown away.

cotton fibre

seed head

stem

◄ Memphis stands on a high bluff overlooking the Mississippi. The city's raised position helps to protect it from flooding.

Cotton plantations

In the early days, cotton was picked by hand by African slaves. Many lived and worked on large plantations, where they endured terrible hardships and were brutally treated by white overseers. Long after slavery was abolished, black people in the southern states suffered discrimination and abuse. Even today, black communities in the South are among the poorest in the United States.

The effects of slavery

Slavery in the southern states lasted from the 16th to the 19th century, but its effects are still felt in America today. Millions of black Americans are descended from African slaves who worked in the cotton fields. The racism that allowed slavery to flourish is still alive in many parts of the American South.

▶ Slaves worked long days in the hot sun with no breaks and without pay. This photograph from the 1860s shows a slave family in the cotton fields of Savannah, Georgia.

YOU ARE HERE

Heading South

South of Memphis, cotton fields once stretched as far as the eye could see. Nowadays, there are new industries along the river.

Oil and gas

When the cotton industry declined, the southern states of Arkansas, Tennessee and Louisiana became the poorest in America. Then, in the 1960s, oil and natural gas were discovered, and large companies like Exxon and Gulf started drilling in the region.

Since then, many industries have moved into the area. As well as car makers like General Motors and Toyota, there are more than 4,000 companies providing services to the oil industry.

▼ Giant oil refineries and storage depots line the river at Baton Rouge, Louisiana (see opposite). The city also has large sugar refineries and paper mills.

Baton Rouge

About 335 km (552 miles) downriver from Memphis, Baton Rouge is the state capital of Louisiana. Until the 1950s, it was a small port. Then the river was widened and deepened so that it could be used by oil tankers. As the big oil companies started to explore the offshore oil fields in the Gulf of Mexico, Baton Rouge became one of the biggest ports in the USA.

Today, the river between Baton Rouge and New Orleans is lined with industrial plants. Because of pollution leaks and the haze of industrial fumes that hangs over it, the area has become known as the 'Chemical Corridor'.

▲ A cargo boat heads downriver to the port of Baton Rouge.

The 'red stick'

The name 'Baton Rouge' comes from French words meaning 'red stick'. The red stick was a mysterious marker that was found by a French sea captain sailing up the Mississippi in 1699. The marker stood on the first high ground along the river. It was here that Baton Rouge was founded, as a small wooden fort overlooking the river.

The River Delta

As you reach the low-lying marshes around New Orleans, the river slows and widens to form a giant, steamy wetland. This is the Mississippi Delta.

YOU ARE HERE

▼ The Louisiana Bayous were formed when the river burst its banks, flooding neighbouring woodland. These tough evergreen trees are mangroves.

The Bayous

At the tip of the delta, a long 'neck' of marshy land stretches out into the sea. On either side are the swampy backwaters known as the Louisiana Bayous. These are a rich habitat for alligators, raccoons, otters, muskrats and black bears. The swamps also provide a summer haven for thousands of migrating wild ducks from the north.

◀ These delta wetlands are a rich habitat for wildlife. They also provide a vital natural defence against storms and tidal waves.

The changing river

Because of silt build-up, the Mississippi's route to the Gulf is constantly changing. Scientists predict that if flood defences fail, the river will leave its present course through Baton Rouge and New Orleans and find a more direct route to the Gulf, either via the Atchafalya River or Lake Pontchartrain (see map).

A threatened landscape

Not long ago, silt from the Mississippi added one square kilometre of land to the delta every two years. Today, saltwater is invading the swamps, forcing out freshwater fish and slowly eroding the coastline.

Another threat is pollution from oil spills. One of the worst was the Deepwater Horizon spill in 2010, when oil from below the seabed poured ashore following an explosion on a British Petroleum (BP) oil rig. Millions of fish and seabirds were contaminated. Local people and relief agencies are still working to repair the damage to the environment and the local economy.

▼ Mississippi alligators were once hunted for their skin. Today, they are a protected species.

New Orleans

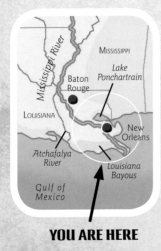

YOU ARE HERE

Your journey ends with a visit to New Orleans. This amazing city has survived floods, wars and tropical storms to become a melting pot of people and cultures from all over the world.

▼ *New Orleans is known as the 'Crescent City' because of its location on a bend of the Mississippi.*

New Orleans was the first town built on the Mississippi, and it is the delta's most important city. It became a settlement because it lay at the mouth of the river, and controlled the only trade route into the country. Most of the city lies below the river's flood level.

levée

◄ Floodwalls and drainage channels are vital to protect New Orleans from flooding. This levée has been rebuilt and strengthened following Hurricane Katrina.

Hurricane Katrina

Because New Orleans is low-lying, it is very vulnerable to flooding. In August 2005, a powerful tropical storm swept across the Gulf of Mexico, creating a huge tide of water that overwhelmed the city's flood defences. A total of 1,863 people died in the disaster, making it one of the worst in US history.

Today, New Orleans is a busy port and an important cultural and tourist centre, but it also struggles with high unemployment, poverty and crime. Many people here are still trying to rebuild their lives after the terrible floods that struck the city in the wake of Hurricane Katrina in 2005.

Customs and cultures

During its history, many different peoples settled in New Orleans. This mixture of cultures gives it a unique atmosphere. It is now home to 1.2 million people, including African-Americans and groups descended from early French and Spanish settlers, known as Creoles.

▶ A street performer plays jazz on the Mississippi waterfront.

Glossary

bluff a steep hill or cliff overlooking a river

channel the shape formed by the banks and bed of a river

confluence a meeting of two rivers

contaminate to spoil, damage or poison

course the route followed by a river

delta an area of marshy land where a river flows out to sea

discrimination unfair treatment

divert to steer or channel away from

dredger a boat used to scoop sediment from the bed of a river

evergreen a type of tree that does not shed its leaves

fertile good for growing

floodplain the area affected by a river's floodwaters

fume harmful gas or vapour

glacier a slow-moving mass of ice

gorge a steep, rocky river valley

habitat the natural home of a plant or animal

harvest to gather or collect a crop

haven a safe place

hazard a danger or obstacle

hurricane a violent tropical storm

hydroelectricity energy generated by flowing water

immigrant a person who moves to another country to start a new life

irrigate to pipe or pump water to a field

levée a sloping wall or bank built to prevent flooding

livestock farm animals such as cows or sheep

lumber felled trees

mammal an animal that gives milk to feed its young

migrate to move from one place to another

pioneer someone who sets out to make a new life in unknown or dangerous territory

prairie flat or gently rolling grassland found in North America

raccoon furry mammal found in North America

refinery a place where oil is processed

reserve an area of land that is set aside for a special purpose

reservoir an artificial lake in which water is stored

saturated full of water

sediment broken-down rocks and stones carried downstream by a river

settler a person who builds a home in new surroundings (see also **pioneer**)

silt fine sediment carried downstream by a river

slave a person who is 'owned' by another and forced to work without pay

source the place where a river begins

stern wheel the rotating paddle of a Mississippi steamboat

talon the sharp claws of a bird or animal

tepee (also **tipi**) a traditional Native American tent

trek a long or difficult overland journey

tributary a stream or river that flows into another, larger one

waterwheel a wooden wheel turned by a stream or river

wharf (*pl*. **wharves**) a place beside a river where goods are unloaded

Mississippi Quiz*

Find the answers in this book, or look them up online.

1 Match the captions to the pictures.

1

2

3

4

5

6

A A Mississippi towboat

B A raccoon

C A mangrove tree

D A Native American tepee

E A waterwheel

F An oil rig

2 These places can all be found along the Mississippi. Place them in order, starting with the ones furthest from the sea:

Memphis
Minneapolis
Baton Rouge
New Orleans
St Louis
Lake Itasca

3 True or false?

'The Mississippi is the longest river in the United States.'

4 Mississippi trappers hunted this animal for its fur. What is it?

*Answers on page 32.

Websites and Further Reading

Websites

- *www.riverworksdiscovery.org*
  Lively and informative site exploring America's waterways
- *www.nps.gov/miss/forkids/index.htm*
  Fun facts and activities about the Mississippi
- *http://discovery.mnhs.org/ConnectingMN/*
  Interactive site exploring the history of Minneapolis and its people

Further reading

Mississippi (Rivers Through Time/ Settlements series) Rob Bowden (Heinemann, 2006)

The Mississippi: America's Mighty River (Rivers Around the World series) Robin Johnson (Crabtree, 2010)

Index

Answers to Mississippi Quiz
1 1D, 2B, 3A, 4C, 5F, 6E. **2** Lake Itasca, Minneapolis, St Louis, Memphis, Baton Rouge, New Orleans. **3** False. The Missouri is longer. **4** A North American beaver.